# FIVE MINUTES FROM A MELTDOWN

*In loving memory of Dana Joy.*

ISBN: 978-1-957262-81-9
***Five Minutes from a Meltdown: A Comedic Poetry and Cartoon Collection***



Yorkshire Publishing
2488 E 81st St.
Ste 2000
Tulsa, OK 74137
www.YorkshirePublishing.com
918.394.2665

Printed in Canada.

A COMEDIC POETRY COLLECTION

# FIVE MINUTES FROM A MELTDOWN

DAVID MEYER

ILLUSTRATED BY MARK HILL

*Thank you to:*

*My parents, for everything they've given me already and all they continue to give me—more than I can ever begin to be grateful enough for.*

*All of my friends and extended family, for their ongoing love, support, and laughter.*

*My great collaborators, Mark, Serena, Kent, and Laura, who helped my poetry come to print and come to life.*

*My English teachers throughout the years (Monsell, Hirsch, Geuder, Forrester, and the particularly poetically-inspiring Berger-White) who all encouraged me, honed my writing, and taught me how to write creatively (something they hopefully don't regret after reading this) and all the other great teachers in the world.*

*My Bens, my writers group, my cousin Carol, Sasha, Rocky, other Sasha, Kelley, and Shel.*

*To everyone else who should be thanked who I forgot or neglected to mention,*

1. *I'm sorry. This is awkward.*
2. *Thank you so much.*

*To everyone who reads this book: Seriously, thank you. I'm incredibly grateful. I hope you enjoy it.*

# CONTENTS

# INTRODUCTION

This is
not
a book
of poetry.
I am
not
a poet.
But,
I
do
love
goofy spacing
to change the
cadence,
so
Here
We
Go.

# ANTHEMS

The man performed at shows
across the world,
with his repertoire of
national anthems,
one after the other.
Guatemala,
China,
Portugal,
Australia,
and more.
He played to sold-out crowds,
to the dismay
of Luke Bryan
and Blake Shelton,
and even the slower-to-anger angel
Dolly Parton.
The National Anthem Tourer
became the number one
best-selling artist
in Country Music.

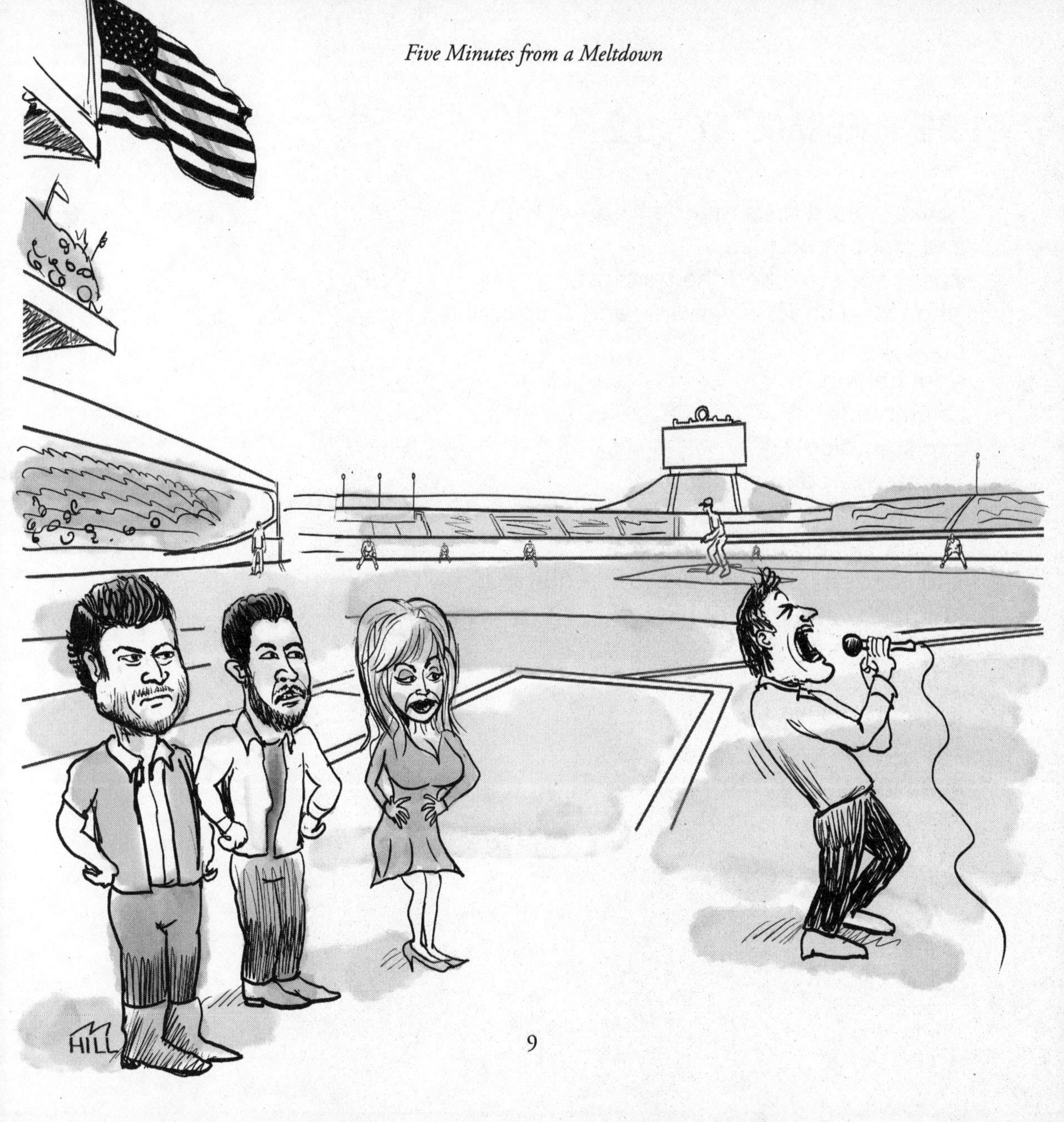
HILL

# THE MESSAGE TO U2

I once waited for a meet-and-greet with U2
and I met Bono first.
But as I approached the guitarist,
who stood under a very low and sharp railing,
I was shoved
from behind.
I stumbled
and stumbled,
but recovered my balance,
ducking below the sharp railing above
in a shockingly athletic move,
and I ended up right next to the guitarist.
I turned to the man behind me
and requested,
"Don't push me
'cause I'm close to
The Edge,
and I'm trying not to
lose my head."

# BASED ON A TRUE STORY

"Mom?"
a pause.
"Mom?"
another pause.
"Mom?"
a momentary silence.
"Mom?"
This went on for
a long time,
breaking the quiet of the night
and the sleep
of the parents.
After many
unanswered calls,
out rang the word
"Dad?"
The mother turned over to
her loving husband.
"The kid wants you,"
she said
and rolled back over
to blissful sleep.

# NOT GETTING MARRIED TODAY

My friend requested
that I bring the wedding bands
to her marriage ceremony.
Imagine my surprise
when I arrived
to find that
she meant
I should bring
the rings.
Imagine my sorrow
when I had to break the news
to the musicians
I had brought.
I helped them load their equipment
back into their respective vans.

"WHAT DO YOU MEAN? THE WEDDING BANDS AREN'T IN YOUR POCKET?"

# FOLKS

Whenever I deliver
baked goods that
my mother
made,
I am always
cautious
and
considerate
regarding those with
allergies.
So I preface with
"These
homemade
baked goods
are processed
in a facility that contains
nuts.
And those
nuts
are
My Parents!"

# THE GOOD OL' DAYS

"Now clap!"
said the grandpa,
ending the dirty joke.
The father leaned over and said,
"Pops,
you can't tell little James
dirty jokes."
The grandpa replied,
"He's a smart boy,
I'm sure
he can understand them."
The father said,
"No, Pops,
it's because they're
inappropriate."
The grandpa simply said
"Oh,"
and returned to thinking about
how much better it was
back in Korea.

# HEAR TODAY, GONE TOMORROW

A deaf man was offered
the opportunity
to hear,
for the first time,
through a technologically advanced machine.
And when they plugged it in,
his world was changed,
but sadly, he heard
your mixtape
and has requested to become deaf again.

THIS IS THE MIXTAPE...
HILL

# THE DEBATE

My father loves
ice cream.
And I love
my father.
I want to make him happy,
so I often think about getting him
a gift of
ice cream.
But
I also want him to
live longer.
And giving him
more dessert
would probably be
counterproductive
to that goal.
So I settle on a
kiddie scoop.

## WELL, WELL, WELL

I knew a man
whose father passed away
and left him only
a water pump in a field.
But the gift served two purposes,
unbeknownst to the dead father.
One,
the man now had fresh water
for his property.
Two,
and perhaps more useful,
rumors began to spread around town
about this man and how he was
well endowed.

# KIDS LIKE THE DARNDEST THINGS

Children will take one
random
thing and make it their entire personality.
At some point
in childhood,
a child might think,
"I love mail. I love it."
And the parents have to now
take their child to
the post office
or to talk to
the mailman
or the child hears, somehow,
(they have no internet access
or really any other notable
resources to find out about such a thing)
about a
mail museum
in Bumblefuck,
Kentucky,
and the parents must schlep them there,
only to discover
when they arrive
that the child now only likes
turtles.

I ♥ U.S. MAIL
HILL

# MY BIGGEST FEAR. ASK MY EXES

I saw that movie
*One Flew Over the Cuckoo's Nest.*
And I saw
*American Horror Stories: Asylum.*
And I saw
*Shutter Island*
and other movies
about
insane asylums and
mental hospitals.
And now, I am afraid
of
commitment.

# CHILDHOOD DREAMS

As far back as I can remember,
I always wanted to be
a gangster.
In fact,
I used to put
pebbles
in my friend's
bathing suit pockets
and throw him in
the deep end
of the pool
and say,
"Tonight,
you a-sleep with the
chlorine."

# WATCH YOUR (RING)TONE

It was at the grocery store
in the bread aisle,
or perhaps the cereal,
that the woman's phone
rang out
next to me.
Her ringtone was
familiar
and took barely even a second to become
recognizable.
The song was
"I Like to Move It,"
by will.i.am,
the song featured in the hit animated film
*Madagascar*.
This ringtone did not ring in 2005,
when said movie was still popular.
It rang in 2021,
when said movie was not
(dare I say)
still popular.
Nevertheless, this woman danced.
Indeed, she let the ringtone ring.

She didn't even check
who was calling,
she simply *moved it, moved it,*
as the singer chanted that *moving*
*it* was indeed what he liked to do.
It was only as she gyrated her hips

that I saw the teenage boy next to her,
certainly her son,
burying his face in his palms
in embarrassment,
and I decided to join in
*moving it, moving it*
with her.

"I LIKE TO MOVE IT MOVE IT!"

# KIDS SAY THE DARNDEST THINGS

I eavesdrop
often
and
have heard
many
funny things,
but none has
stuck with me
quite like
the two kids
who sat in the restaurant booth
next to mine
in which
one said,
"Her mother is a CFO,"
to which
the other replied,
"She's a flying saucer?"

# HEY, YOU ASKED

I got into
an accident
with a truck
that had a sign
on the back,
asking
"How is my driving?"
with a number to call.
It was
his fault,
so I called.
He was,
apparently,
the truck business owner,
so he picked up
the phone.
I said,
"Not good!"

# SIGNS

"Drive like your family lives here"
signs
severely underestimate
how badly
I'd like to hit my family
with a fast-moving vehicle.
What? It's a joke!

DRIVE LIKE
YOUR FAMILY
LIVES HERE
HILL

# YOUR DUMB

I met a man once
who was so dumb
that I could hear him out loud
use the wrong form of
"their"
in a sentence.

# VILLAGES

It takes a village,
I was told,
and
every village
has its idiot,
I was told,
and
it takes one to know one,
I was told.
So, if you don't know
who the idiot
in your village is,
it must be you.

# WHEN YOU CAN SEE THIS FUTURE, I GET IT

I want to find a
happy medium,
but
every psychic
I visit
seems very
miserable.

JACK
ZODIAC
PSYCHIC
HILL

# STATS

That fact
that the average person
eats eight spiders
in their sleep
each year
is misleading
because
the truth is
there is only one man,
the Sleep-Spider-Eater-Man,
who eats 64 billion spiders
in his sleep each year.
And that,
my dear pupils,
is why averages
are unreliable statistics.
Class dismissed.

IT'S STRANGE HOW I ALWAYS WAKE UP FEELING FULL, WITH NO INTEREST IN BREAKFAST.
BELCH
HILL

# SCHOOL'S OUT

I once went to
an event
where they decided
the winner
of a competition
by crowd noise.
When one side
was up,
the other side
booed,
which is not helpful
to your cause
in a noise-based
competition.
Our education
system
has failed.

# YOUTH

I feel just terrible
about how long I laughed
at the young man
next to me
at the pharmacy counter
who held up the
box of condoms
he was purchasing
and,
in a moment of
nervousness,
offered up,
"Don't worry,
they're not for me;
they're for my dad."

# STOLE

I once got my
pocket picked
when I was in college.
I was carrying some
cash
and
gift cards
and
my IDs
and
insurance card
and
credit card
in
my wallet.
While I was
disappointed
and
livid
and
frustrated,
I knew I could check
where

my credit card was being used.
To comfort myself,
I hoped that my robber needed
the money
more than I did.
The rest was
replaceable,
more or less.
When I checked
where
my robber had gone to spend
my money,
I saw that he had gone to
Lids,
the hat and sports store.
Not to a
grocery store
or
pharmacy
or
anywhere else where I could have
convinced myself
that he needed my money

to survive.
No.
This robber went to
Lids
and tried to charge, on
my credit card,
four hundred dollars' worth of
Patriots jerseys
and other assorted gear.
My pocket was
picked,
and I remain
pissed
pertaining to this
purloining
pilfering
Patriots
prick.

# TOUGH NEWS

The customer is always right.
It's true,
which was hard for me to swallow,
especially when one of them
told me
that I was
an idiot.

# FULL OF THEMSELVES

I went to a
Narcissists Anonymous
meeting,
but it
never
got past
the introductions.

NARCISSISTS
ANONYMOUS
INTRODUCTIONS
ZZZZZZ
ZZZZZ
HILL

# MAYBE MY FAVORITE POEM I'VE EVER WRITTEN

I had a dog
that I adopted.
At night,
it would murmur
"I climbed Mt. Everest."
Between snores,
it would say,
"I beat Muhammad Ali
in a boxing match."
In the darkness,
it would exclaim,
"I did not have
sexual relations
with that woman."
I took this dog
to the vet,
who simply told me
it was
no big deal,
insisting that I
"Let sleeping dogs lie."

I DATED LASSIE
I WON THE IDITAROD!
I INVENTED BITCOIN.
THAT DOES IT. I'M MOVING HIM DOWNSTAIRS.
EASY, HON. REMEMBER WHAT THE VET SAID ABOUT SLEEPING DOGS.
HILL

# A POEM I WROTE A WHILE AGO BUT WAS REMINDED OF AGAIN TODAY BY A CONVERSATION WITH MY LOVELY MOTHER

I don't listen to
podcasts.
But
I have another
tactic.
A podcast can range from
thirty minutes
to
an hour,
or even longer.
Luckily,
I have parents
who listen to podcasts.
And they
call me up
and can tell me
all about
the podcast they just listened to,
in only
three

hours.
"What
a
deal,"
I tell myself,
as I pace
around
my apartment,
lacing the cord around my neck.

# I'M THE NEXT GREAT SUPERVILLAIN

If I was fighting Spider-Man,
I would simply make my
suit
and
my lair
and
everything else that was pertinent
out of the
same material
that they make
non-stick pans.

## MOST PEOPLE REJECTED HIS MESSAGE. THEY HATED HIM BECAUSE HE TOLD THEM THE TRUTH.

Who convinced
the world that
indoor skydiving
was a form of
skydiving?
Where is
the sky?
Indoor skydiving
is just
diving,
and I'm only
slightly
afraid to say it.

# ROUND AND ROUND WE GO

I saw a
NASCAR driver
in a
cul-de-sac
recently.
Logic tells me
he may
still
be there.

# SAGE ADVICE

I knew a wise man
once,
and
that wise man told me
"
."
Because sometimes
the wisest thing to say is
nothing
at all.

Ø
HILL

# THE MAN AT PEACE

I sat next to
a man
on a
plane.
On this
plane,
there was
a baby.
It cried
and cried,
but how could I
begrudge it
or its mother?
I did not
blame either one.
But I envied
the man
next to me.
For he had
noise-cancelling
headphones.
I did not.
I heard

this baby
scream
and
cry
for hours.
I tapped
the man
on the shoulder,
and he raised
one headphone.
"You're lucky to have those
noise-cancelling
headphones,"
I said.
He nodded.
"What are you listening to
instead of this
racket,
if you don't mind
my asking?"
He pondered the question,
to decide
if he minded,

then took his
headphones off
and put them on
my ears,
revealing
to me
that he was listening to
the sounds of
babies
crying.

# I'M SORRY, REALLY

I went to an
Irish pub
and ordered
an
Irish car bomb.
The
bartender
shook her head in
disappointment
and
anger
and told me that I was
insensitive.
After all,
didn't I know that
her cousin
had died
while drinking an
Irish car bomb?

# BEST IN TOWN

I saw a
cute
little
diner
on the side of the road.
In bright
neon lights
the diner boasted,
"Best
patty melt
in town
since 1945."
I was
impressed,
but then
I found out
they had been serving
patty melts
since 1910.
Now,
I simply wonder
what they
changed

about their patty melts
in '44.

# TRADITION

I reached
for my wallet
when the bill came.
They laughed
so hard
they cried
at my attempt.
For what friend's parents
have ever allowed
the friend to actually pay for dinner?
I sighed in relief
that, once again,
my attempt had failed.
I dread the day
when they say,
"Yes, you can pay."
Then, they will see
that,
despite this charade
of attempting to
pay for my share,
I don't actually carry
any money

in my wallet.
For what friend's parents have
ever
allowed the friend to
actually
pay for dinner?

# CHARCUTERIE IS SERVED ON BOARDS ABOVE WOOD, NOT UNDERWOOD

Jesus was throwing a party
and was making a
charcuterie board.
He had the meats picked out,
he could make the wine from water,
but he couldn't decide how much
cheese
to buy from the store.
When he asked the expert behind
the fromagerie counter,
the man said,
"Jesus, take the wheel."

# REWATCHABLES

My friend is
very bad
at predicting things
in movies.
He is
always
surprised,
even by the
most quotidian
plots,
most predictable
events,
most mundane
twists.
But, to his credit,
he can usually tell
when a character will die
when he watches the movie
for a
second time.

# PICKUP LINES

I go to the
bar
with my friends.
I go around with my
usual
pickup line.
I approach
a girl
and I say,
"Hey
girl,
are you from
Tennessee?"
and if she says,
"No,"
I move on,
until I find
a girl
from
Tennessee.
Then,
I already have
a conversation starter.

NO, I'M NOT FROM TENNESSEE.
ARE *YOU* FROM TENNESSEE?
HILL

# JURY'S OUT

I once
got dozens upon dozens
of letters in my mailbox
over a long period of time,
requesting my presence in court
to serve my country
and my duty
on a jury.
I ignored each and every
one of these letters,
until one day
a policeman showed up at my door
and arrested me
and took me to court
and held me in custody
to be tried
for not showing up for my jury duty.
I despaired,
and begged,
and worried,
but
lucky me,
it seems that I was not alone

in my reluctance,
and indignation,
and laziness,
about serving jury duty,
as no one showed
up to serve theirs
for my trial,
and thus there was no jury
to try me for my crime.
I was let go.
A lesson was learned,
but I'm not sure it was a good one.

# MY SIDE GIG

I recently got a job
working the desk at a bank,
dealing solely with clients
who have amassed a great deal of wealth.
When asked about it,
I realized
that my current title
is not actually
"Desk Worker for the Rich,"
as I thought,
but is more accurately called
"Fortunes Teller."

FORTUNES TELLER

# BATH-IN-TIME

My shower recently entered a
dance competition.
It had each part participate in a different
style of dance.
The showerhead did the tango.
The handles danced contemporary.
The shower caddy competed in breakdancing.
The Irish Spring soap performed … well, Irish dancing.
The tub had ballroom.
The door did swing.
And
of course,
the drain clogged.

# GIVING THANKS

I had some hard times.
I dealt with some tough troubles.
I was an addict.
I couldn't go a day without thinking about it.
That thing that took me away from everyday life—
The Butterball—
was all I could think about.
But I had some great support.
Some really close friends who cared for me.
Finally, through hard work,
support systems, like the Butterball Hotline,
and
a lot more,
I finally quit Cold Turkey.

# CLEAN AS A WHAT?

Who
on earth
saw someone
blowing
spittle and
moisture
and all other
kinds of mouth-germ-things
through
a whistle,
and then created
an expression
using it as the
pinnacle
of Cleanliness?

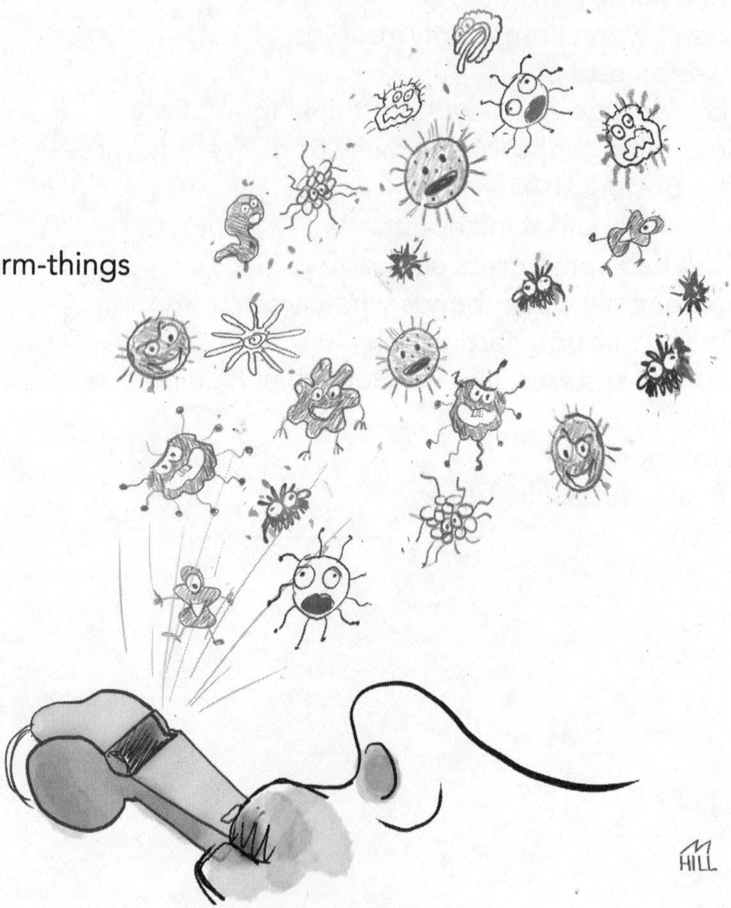

# EVERYONE'S A CRITIC

Say what you will
about me,
but
only
if they're
good things.

# WELL, THAT'S JUST BAD LUCK

My friend
smoked weed
a week
before a drug test
for his job.
This was not a
pee test;
this was a
hair test,
so no cleansing routine
would help.
He panicked,
rightfully so,
even though
drug tests,
particularly for weed,
are stupid.
He bought
a wig
of real hair.
And,
what bad luck,
the original grower

of the hair
had done more
cocaine than
Scarface.

# INSTRUCTIONS NOT INCLUDED

I am
a simple man.
I am
a very good listener.
But
I am
not a great dancer.
I am
thus
a fan of songs
with instructions.
I may be lost
during any other song,
my limbs
flailing
hopelessly,
my body
swaying
awkwardly.
But when
the
"Electric Slide"
or

"Time Warp"
or
"Cupid Shuffle"
comes on,
watch me
tear up
the floor
with the well-informed,
proper
dance moves.
"To the left,"
you say?
To the left
I shall be.

# SALTY, SALTY

Have you heard the tales
of those people who see
Jesus Christ
in their crackers?
They keep the crackers
as a sign of faith,
or they sell them
as a sign of prosperity,
all because of an unusual
shape or marking.
Now, I'm not a religious man,
nor do I think Jesus would ever bless
me in particular,
so when I saw the shape in my cracker,
it blew me away.
But I did not see the Lord and Savior.
No,
I got a much,
much
worse alternative:
A Russian-dictating oligarch.
I eyed my cracker with great detail,
almost touching the salt with my eyelids,

and my suspicion was,
sadly,
confirmed.
There,
upon my cracker,
an image of
Putin on the Ritz.

# EVERY TIME

"Why didn't
you
invite me
to your
surprise
party?"
he interrogated.
"It was a
surprise
party
for me,"
I implored.
"We're
friends.
Why didn't
you
invite me?"
He asked.
It hit me
then.
"You think
I
planned my own

surprise
party?"
What an
idiot
my
best
friend is.

# HELLO KITTY

I did not realize that they used to keep
cats
in bags.
I did not realize that keeping
cats
in bags
was
a secret.
But alas,
it was
a secret
when one carried a
cat
in a bag.
Thus,
if it escaped,
then
your secret
was out,
and the cat was
out of the bag.

# EARLY TO YOUR OWN FUNERAL

If you
ask me,
calling a
dead person
"late"
is a
dumb
term.
I
hate
to tell you this,
but that person
isn't late;
they're
probably
not
going to be
showing up
at all.

# FOR YOUR NEXT INSULT BATTLE

I hope
that you
get
a headache
right before
your favorite band's concert
and no one around you
has Tylenol.
I hope the next time you're on a plane you
get
the middle seat
between a stinky person,
who has gas from the tinned sardines
they're still eating,
and an ill person,
making the most use of their
puke bag.
If you were a chicken
you would be a jerk chicken.
I'm sorry. I didn't mean it.
You'll always be my favorite aunt.

SARDINES
HILL

# NOT BETTING ON A SECOND ONE

I was at
a coffee shop
the other day
and saw a first date
occurring.
I knew
that,
besides the coffee,
trouble
was also
brewing
when the man arrived
first
and got his
coffee.
When his date
arrived,
ordered,
and paid,
he said,
"Oh, shoot,"
regarding him
not being polite by

paying for
her coffee.
Instead, he
handed her
a five-dollar-bill
and said,
"It's on me."

# THE STONE-COLD TRUTH

"Come see our famous rock"
"It's called butt rock"
"It's called skull rock"
"Because it looks like a butt"
"Because it looks like a skull,"
said every National Park employee,
as pretty much every sprawling landscape
consisting of rocks
will have one that looks like a butt
and one that looks like a skull
if that's what you're looking for.

THAT'S A LETDOWN. THOSE ROCKS AREN'T SHAPED LIKE EASTER EGGS.
YEAH. DUDE. LET'S READ THE BROCHURE AGAIN.
HILL

# A NEW AGE

"Scan this QR code for my Linktree."
So said the unhoused man,
as he held up his piece of cardboard,
a QR code etched into the material.
I'd have given him a five,
had I had any cash,
but I had none,
so instead,
I scanned,
which worked,
to my surprise,
because the QR was hand-drawn,
and
I did not give him five dollars.
No,
not even one.
But instead,
I downloaded
the man's newest single
on Spotify
and subscribed
to his OnlyFans.

"JUST SCAN THE QR CODE."

# LET'S DISH

I refuse to do
the dishes.
I've refused
before,
but then, I admit,
I did give in.
And the dishes were done,
by yours truly,
at that.
But no more!
That was a
different
time.
Today is not yesterday nor yesterday's tomorrow.
It is tomorrow's yesterday,
and I will make today a day to be
remembered tomorrow!
The dishes will remain in the sink.
I won't even turn on the water,
not let it rinse half-assed over the plates and silverware.
I won't let it pool in a bowl.
Even to do
that

would be
beneath
my dignity and
above
my pay grade.
I hope you like your dishes
dirty,
because they're going to stay that way, like it or not!
I don't care.
I don't.
Really.
I'll eat my future meals off dirty porcelain, tasting the
memories
of past meals as left to me
through
unidentified
stains
and lumps
and chunks.
If you won't do the same,
why don't you do the dishes, then, huh?
Why don't you?
Why is it always my job?

Oh, right.
I live
alone.
Fuck.
Guess I'd better grab the sponge.

# THINGS TO REMEMBER

- To turn the lights off when you leave a room
- To use your turn signals while driving
- Loved ones' birthdays
- Those who supported you in tough times
- To clean the dishes as you go
- To like and subscribe
- When you put something in the oven
- The Alamo
- Why you made that risky decision
- Where you came from
- To tip your waiters
- That one time? Ha, that was super funny!
- The punchline before you start to tell the joke
- The little guys when you're big
- Your social security number. Mine is—
- To check your closet and under the bed for monsters and dust bunnies
- The tiny variations of that one password you use for everything
- Which identical twin you are dating
- To drink water and stay hydrated

- That who you were yesterday does not define who you are today or will be tomorrow
- The hardest lessons you've had to learn, so you don't need to relearn them
- To check your pockets for your wallet, keys, and phone
- To call the people you love and tell them that
- Nothing matters in the long term
- But, in the short term, the previous statement doesn't matter either
- Who you want to be to the world
- Who you want to be to yourself